TWELVE MIRRORS

TWELVE MIRRORS
A System of Perception
by J. A. Gucci

TWELVE MIRRORS: *A System of Perception*
(Standard Edition). Copyright © 2026 J. A. Gucci
All rights reserved.

No part of this publication may be reproduced, distributed, or transmitted in any form or by any means—including electronic, mechanical, photocopying, recording, or otherwise—without the prior written permission of the publisher, except in the case of brief quotations used in reviews, educational contexts, or scholarly analysis.

This book presents a structured poetic system intended for creative and instructional use. Readers, educators, and students are encouraged to engage with, interpret, and respond to the material; however, the original text and its compositional framework remain the intellectual property of the author.

Published by Pressure System Press

Printed in the United States of America

First edition, 2026

ISBN: 978-1-972788-13-4

www.jagucci.com

CONTENTS

PREFACE

These poems originate in observable phenomena
rather than symbolic invention. Each mirror
presents a physical system at the precise moment
perception undergoes structural transformation.
Drawn from optics, meteorology, hydrology,
astronomy, geology, and biology, the compositions
isolate conditions under which ordinary
appearances become temporarily unstable.

The sequence is organized as twelve distinct
mirrors of perception. Every poem is governed by a
triadic progression through which an initial state
encounters a transforming condition before
arriving at a new perceptual outcome. Rather than
explaining these processes, the poems reduce them
to their observable consequences, allowing each
system to emerge through its own internal
correspondence.

Nothing within these pages asks to be decoded.
The poems simply invite sustained observation.
Their meanings do not precede the structures from
which they arise; they emerge through the
relationships that remain visible upon the page.

HOW TO READ THIS BOOK

Read each poem slowly before attempting to
explain it.

Notice what is physically present. Observe where a
condition changes, where a boundary is crossed, or
where an appearance begins to shift. Resist the
impulse to translate the images into symbols.
Instead, follow the observable relationships that
connect one state to the next.

Many of the systems presented here are drawn
directly from the natural world. The poems
intentionally omit the explanatory mechanisms that
produce these transformations while preserving
their visible consequences. As a result, the reader is
invited to reconstruct the continuity of the system
through careful observation rather than
interpretation.

Return often. Like the phenomena they describe,
these mirrors frequently reveal additional
structural relationships through repeated attention.

*"Nothing here will change.
What you see will."*

Mirror I: Misrecognition

Still cove
saw-toothed slope

upside
down

smooth.

Mirror II: Doubt

Jutting black
stack

settled on silt
brooding,

cool—
buoy

Mirror III: Belief

Frozen grey
rock

settling—

red
pink moon.

.

Mirror IV: Entanglement

Songbird streaking
moon

light,
floodlight—

loops.

Mirror V: Recognition

Moon over dew

crisscrossed—

shattered.

Mirror VI: Projection

Streaking sunbeam
skewed

clam
buried in the bed

alight on the surface.

Mirror VII: Reconstruction

Spring tide

undulating
calm

crest.

Mirror VIII: Trace

Yellow sky
dry

duff
strike!

turpentine air.

Mirror IX: Revision

Spring rain
pond

gleaming shallow
bed

burrows.

Mirror X: Dissolution

Sun
between a sun
a sun—

rainbow.

Mirror XI: Recursion

Slot canyon walls
calm

black river—

calm
slot canyon walls.

Mirror XII: No Self

Grey flamingo
brine krill—

pink.

APPENDIX: PRINCIPLES OF ABSOLUTE COMPOSITION

The poems in this volume were composed according to the principles of Absolute Composition, a formal methodology that models poetic structure on observable physical systems rather than symbolic association.

Each mirror presents a complete transformation through a triadic relationship consisting of an initial condition, a transforming threshold, and a resulting perceptual state. Rather than explaining the mechanisms that produce these transformations, the compositions preserve only those observable elements necessary for the system to remain structurally complete.

Language is deliberately compressed. Metaphor gives way to correspondence, exposition gives way to observation, and interpretation follows rather than precedes structure. The resulting poems function as formal studies in perception, demonstrating how meaning may emerge directly from the organization of observable relationships.

Readers interested in the complete theoretical framework are encouraged to consult *Absolute Composition*.

THE TWELVE SERIES

Each book in this series presents systems through short, structured poems.

Rather than describing events, the poems model how systems form, interact, and change over time.

Each volume focuses on a different civilization, using the same method to reveal how complex societies develop.

History

Twelve Clay Tablets
Twelve Marble Questions
Twelve Roman Thresholds
Twelve Medieval Thresholds

Creative Writing

Twelve Small Windows
Twelve Loops
Twelve Mirrors
Twelve Rooms

Philosophy

Twelve Iron Paradoxes

ABOUT THE AUTHOR

J. A. Gucci is an educator and writer whose work focuses on systems, structure, and the relationship between form and meaning.

His books present historical and conceptual material through short, structured poems designed to model how systems form and change over time.

COLOPHON

This book was set in a clear, readable typeface to
support careful observation and sustained
attention.

The poems follow a consistent structure to
emphasize pattern, repetition, and continuity over
time.

Designed and produced as part of the Twelve
series.

www.ingramcontent.com/pod-product-compliance
Lightning Source LLC
Chambersburg PA
CBHW021349060726
47591CB00006B/2238